Sophia Shares Her Hope

Kristyn Perez

www.thedailygraceco.com

Unless otherwise noted, Scripture quotations have been taken from the Christian Standard Bible®, Copyright © 2017 by Holman Bible Publishers.
Used by permission. Christian Standard Bible® and CSB® are federally registered trademarks of Holman Bible Publishers.

Designed in the United States of America and printed in China.

STUDY CONTRIBUTORS

Illustrator:
KATIE WILL

Editor:
ALLI TURNER

Sophia is eight, with bright eyes and a smile.
O how she loves family and friends!

She loves cooking and running and playing outside,
Doing cartwheels and crazy back bends.

She's in second grade at Shady Creek School.
She loves science, math, and PE.

Her family loves Jesus, and she's gone to church
Every Sunday since she was just three.

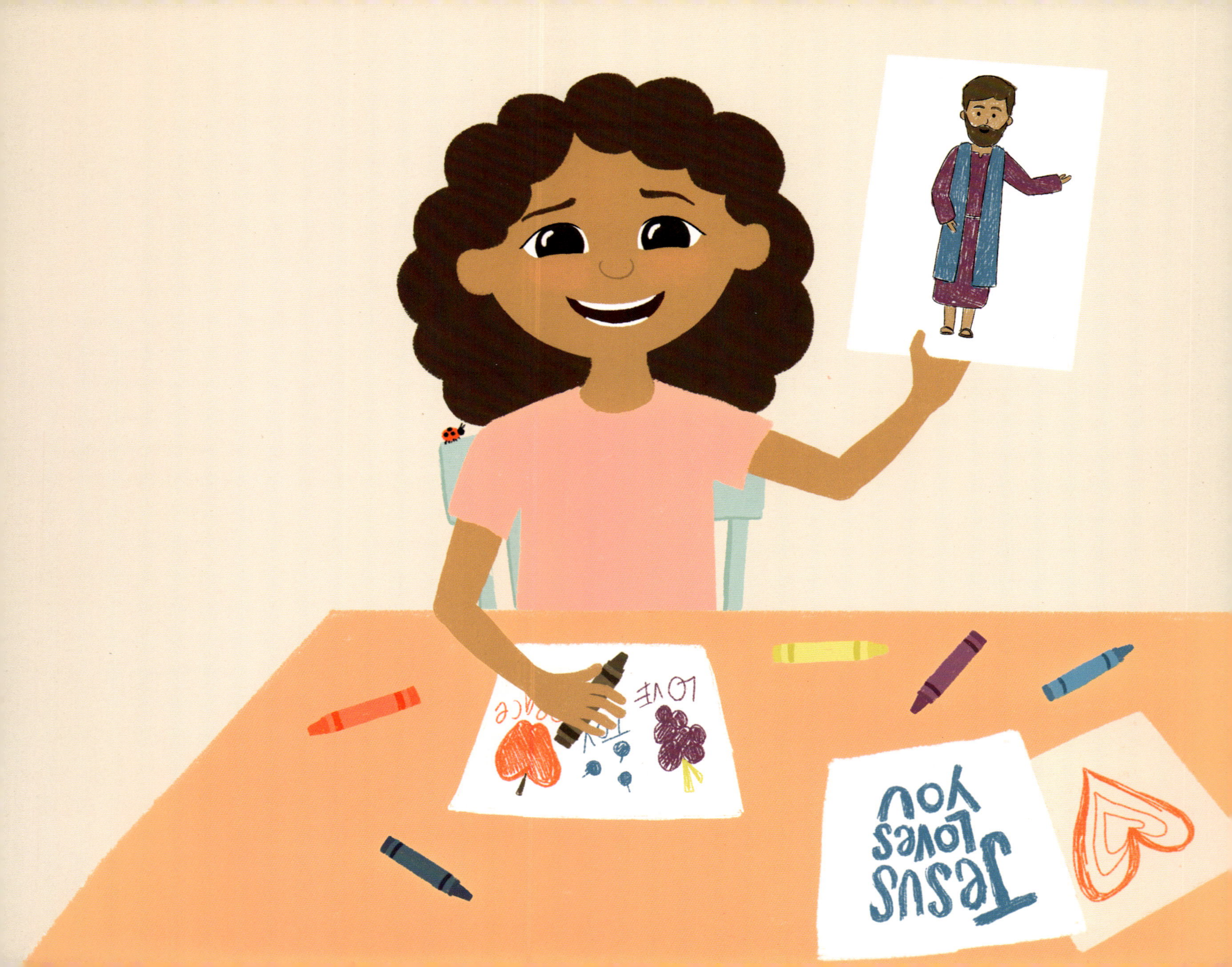
LOVE
Jesus Loves You

Sophia believes that Jesus is God.
She can't leave this news undiscovered.
He fills up her heart with love, joy, and peace.
How could she not share with another?

So one day at school, while playing hopscotch,
Sophia was deep, deep in thought.

She decided right then—she must tell her friends!
She'd share about God on the spot.

So she took a deep breath and said a quick prayer
And decided to share the good news.

As she started to speak, she froze and went still,
Would they believe what she said to be true?

For what if her friends just laugh as she speaks,
And what if they call her mean names?

What if she stutters or stammers or stumbles?
And what if they don't feel the same?

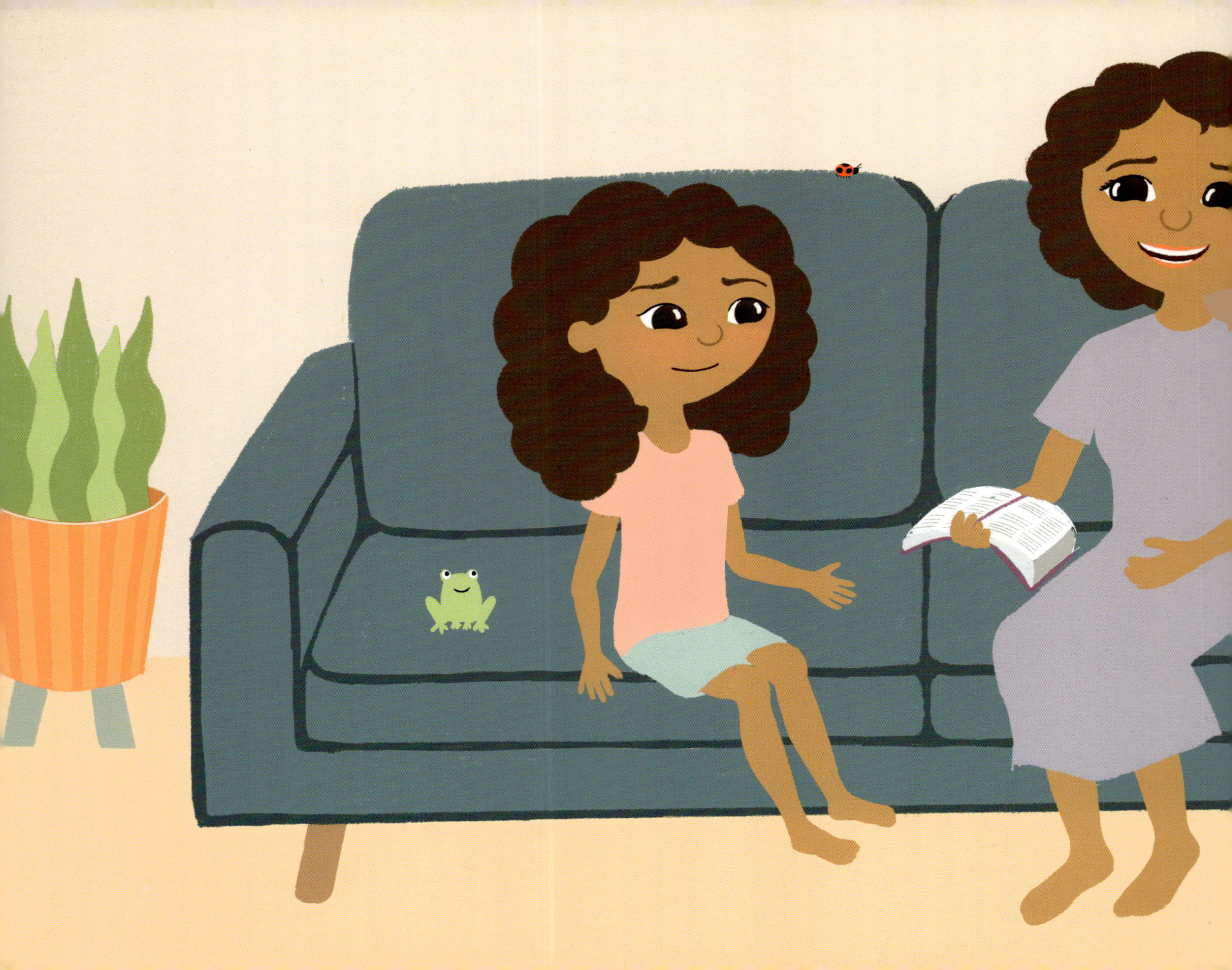

Just then she remembered the words of her mom,
Who first told her of God's great love.
"We're sinners in need of a Savior," she said.
"God's perfect, as pure as a dove."

"God is better than we could imagine.
He's holy and perfect and good.
He wants us to know of His greatness and love,
But we don't love Him like we should."

"God is the best! He loves us so much!
But we turn from Him, and we sin.

We lie, cheat, and steal.
We're mean to our friends.
We have this deep problem within."

"So God sent His Son to live life on Earth.
He ate, drank, and lived perfectly

He died on a cross and took on our sins
For all who would turn and believe."

So Sophia thought back on how life had changed,
Since she trusted Jesus that day,

He became her best friend. He helps her be kind.
He leads her and shows her the way.

"God loves me. He's worthy," she thought to herself. "He's faithful, my great, awesome God.

He's with me, accepts me, and helps me be brave,
Even if friends think I'm odd."

So with this mind, she steadied her step
And looked at her friends, filled with love.

"Can I tell you a story," she asked with a smile,
"Of my God, who is pure from above?"

"He loves you," said Sophia. "He is good, right, and true.
But our sin divides us from Him.
So Jesus came down, and He made a way
For our future to not be so grim."

And as she went on, her friends listened in.
They wondered and pondered and saw,
How great is her God, He's holy and good,
In this greatest story of all.

God is calling His children. He's bringing them home.
He's giving them hope and peace too.

God used Sophia to tell the good news.
Could the next one He uses be you?

What is the Gospel?

THE WORD "GOSPEL" MEANS "GOOD NEWS."

The gospel is the most beautiful story in the whole world! God created the world and everything in it and made it good. He also made people, and He loved them very much.

**BUT THE PEOPLE DISOBEYED GOD.
THIS IS CALLED SIN.**

We all disobey God, and the punishment for our sin is death. Thankfully, God had a plan from the beginning to save His people. We deserve to die for our sins, but the gospel says that God sent His Son, Jesus, to take our place. Jesus, who never sinned, died on the cross for us. Three days later, He came alive again! If we believe this good news and trust Jesus to save us, God forgives us, and we can live forever with Him.

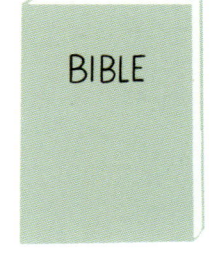

**WHEN WE TRUST IN JESUS,
GOD CHANGES OUR HEARTS.**

He forgives us, makes us clean, and sends His Spirit to live inside us. He makes us His sons and daughters. He protects, loves, and cares for us. In response, we want to live in a way that makes Him happy. Doing good things doesn't save us. We don't obey God to make Him love us. He loves us always and forever! Instead, we obey God because we love Him.

WE CAN LEARN MORE ABOUT GOD AND WHAT HE LOVES THROUGH THE MOST IMPORTANT BOOK OF ALL, THE BIBLE.

The Bible tells us that one day, Jesus is coming again to make everything right. He will wipe away all our tears, and there will be no more pain or sadness. He will make everything good again.

If you trust in Jesus, don't keep this good news to yourself.
Tell someone about Jesus today!

Did you notice our little friends hiding on each page?
Let's read it again and find them!

Thank You

for studying God's
Word with us!

connect with us
@THEDAILYGRACECO @KRISTINSCHMUCKER

contact us
INFO@THEDAILYGRACECO.COM

share
#THEDAILYGRACECO #LAMPANDLIGHT

visit us online
THEDAILYGRACECO.COM